Essentials of
Quality Circles

SHYAM BHATAWDEKAR
Dr KALPANA BHATAWDEKAR

Essentials of
Quality Circles

Books by Shyam Bhatawdekar and Dr Kalpana Bhatawdekar

1. *HSoftware* (Human Software) (The *Only* Key to Higher Effectiveness)
2. Sensitive Stories of Corporate World (Management Case Studies)
3. Classic Management Games, Exercises, Energizers and Icebreakers (Volume 1)
4. Classic Management Games, Exercises, Energizers and Icebreakers (Volume 2)
5. Stress? No Way!! (Handbook on Stress Management)
6. *HSoftware* (Shyam Bhatawdekar's Effectiveness Model)
7. Competencies and Competency Matrix
8. Essentials of Work Study (Method Study and Work Measurement
9. Essentials of Time Management (Taking Control of Your Life)
10. Essentials of 5S Housekeeping
11. Essentials of Quality Circles
12. The Romance of Intimacy
13. Good People (Dream of a Boundary Less World) *Novel, a refreshingly different love story*
14. Funny (and Not So Funny) Short Stories
15. Stories Children Will Love (Volume 1: Bhanu-Shanu-Kaju-Biju and Dholu Ram Gadbad Singh)
16. Travelogue: Scandinavia, Russia

To Our Family

Shyam Bhatawdekar   Dr Kalpana Bhatawdekar

"Quality Circles" is one of the most beneficial Japanese management systems. Large number of organizations all over the world adopted this system due to its significant contribution towards overall organizational improvements.

The salient feature of "Quality Circles" is its facility to involve a large number of people of an organization in the problem solving process and to keep them highly motivated. Thus both- the organization as well its people- benefit in various ways. Its other aspect is its applicability to every kind of organization.

Considering its huge benefits and scope a thorough knowledge of "Quality Circles" becomes imperative. To facilitate gaining the knowledge in this vital subject in the shortest time, authors Shyam Bhatawdekar and Dr Kalpana Bhatawdekar included only the "essentials" of "Quality Circles" in the book.

The authors are top-notch business executives, highly sought after business and management consultants, eminent management gurus, authentic human behavior experts and prolific authors. And so the book becomes an authentic document on the subject.

To read more by the authors, refer their websites: http://shyam.bhatawdekar.com, *http://writings-of-shyam.blogspot.com* and http://management-universe.blogspot.com

Essentials of Quality Circles

Shyam Bhatawdekar
Dr Kalpana Bhatawdekar

Published by Publishing Division of

Prodcons Group

8, Pranjal Society, Shiv Tirth Nagar, Paud Road, Pune
411038 (India)

Email: prodcons@prodcons.com

For other web publications, refer: http://management-
universe.blogspot.com and
http://shyam.bhatawdekar.com

Contents

Essentials of Quality Circles

Brief History of Quality Circles (QC) or Quality Control Circles (QCC)

- Pioneered by Japanese.
- Dr Kaoru Ishikawa of Japan is credited with Quality Circles' inception.
- Japanese nomenclature: Quality Control Circles (QCC), generally now known as Quality Circles (QC) or some call it as Small Group Activity (SGA).
- 1962: First QC Circle was registered with QC Circle Head Quarters in Japan.
- 1974: Lockheed Company, USA started Quality Circle movement.
- 1977: International Association of Quality Circles (IACC) was formed in USA.
- 1980: BHEL, Hyderabad, India- first to start Quality Circles in India.
- 1982: Quality Circle Forum of India (QCFI) was founded.

The history of evolution of Quality Circles in much greater details is appended towards the end of this book.

Formal and Informal Groups

Formal Groups

- Family.
- Organization.
- Departments.

Informal Groups

- Employees meet near water cooler and gossip.
- Five salesmen from marketing department meet once a month for lunch to discuss mutual concerns and to seek relief from tedious aspects of their job.
- Four computer programmers form a jogging club that meets three days a week at lunchtime to run two miles.
- All employees of a section meet and discuss how to improve and beautify office layouts.
- Seven workers of a production shop floor meet once a week to solve their technical problems.

- Maintenance department staff meets regularly to maintain machines in a better way.
- Persons coming from same geographical locations (same town or same country) meet together socially to share and support.

What is Quality Circle (QC)?

Quality Circles are informal voluntary groups of employees working on similar tasks or sharing an area of responsibility who voluntarily meet together on a regular basis to identify, define, analyze and solve work related problems.

Usually and conventionally the members of a particular team (Quality Circle) are from the same work area or who do similar work so that the problems they select will be familiar to all of them. In addition, interdepartmental or cross-functional Quality Circles are also formed.

While the employees may initiate formation of groups informally and voluntarily, soon or during course of their working together as a group they institutionalize their small groups by registering themselves as Quality Circles through organization's formal systems.

While people form the Quality Circles purely voluntarily or because of handholding or prompting by the management (pseudo voluntary in nature) the introduction and promotion of Quality Circles system and formalizing or institutionalizing it in an organization is basically a management decision and responsibility.

Size of a Quality Circle

An ideal size of quality circle is seven to eight members. But the number of members in a Quality Circle can vary depending on the actual requirements.

Other Names of Quality Circles

- Small Groups
- Action Circles
- Excellence Circles
- Human Resources Circles
- Productivity Circles

Basic Premise of Quality Circles

- A person may not always have a right to say "yes" (i.e. the right to take decisions or participate in decision-making or giving ideas and recommendations) but he always has a right to say "no" which he can exercise (and often exercises) by his non-involvement, apathy, disinterest, indifference etc. So why not give him the right to say "yes"?

- People participation in problem solving and decision-making improves the quality of work. More brains are better than one.

- People at every level are often interested in doing a good job.

- People want to be kept informed about the goals and issues of the organizations where they work.

- People want to be recognized as intelligent human beings who are interested to participate in decision-making.

- Employees wish to take up responsibilities and having achieved the results want to be recognized to boost their self-esteem.

Objectives of Quality Circles

- Promote job involvement.
- Create problem solving capability.
- Improve communication.
- Promote leadership qualities.
- Promote personal development.
- Develop a greater awareness for cleanliness.
- Develop greater awareness for safety.
- Improve morale through closer identity of employee objectives with organization's objectives.
- Reduce errors.
- Enhance quality.
- Inspire more effective teamwork.
- Build an attitude of problem prevention.
- Promote cost reduction.
- Develop harmonious manager, supervisor and worker relationship.
- Improve productivity.
- Reduce downtime of machines and equipment.
- Increase employee motivation.

Quality Circle Meetings

- Meetings are important part of Quality Circle's working.
- All the members of the Quality Circle attend meetings.
- In general, meetings take place once a week or once in a fortnight.
- Each meeting lasts for approximately one hour, though variations are possible.
- Apart from the frequency of the meetings, what is important is the regularity of the meetings.

What Takes Place During Quality Circle Meetings?

Any of the several activities may occur during a meeting such as:

- Identifying a theme or a problem to work on.
- Getting/giving training as required enabling members to analyze problem(s).
- Collection of relevant data and information.

15

- Analyzing problem(s).
- Preparing recommendations for implementing solution(s).
- Prepare for a presentation to the management.
- Follow up of implementation of suggestions.

Process of Problem Solving Followed by Quality Circles

Quality Circles use the following steps in the sequence given below for problem solving:

1. Identify the problems.
2. Select the problem out of the identified problems for finding its solution(s).
3. Define the problem.
4. Collect data and analyze the problem. Find the causes of the problem. Try to uncover the root level causes.
5. Generate alternative solutions.
6. Select the best and most appropriate solution(s).
7. Prepare action plan for implementing the solution(s).

8. Seek approval of management by presenting the proposals to the management.
9. Implement the solution(s).
10. Periodically review and control by taking corrective actions.

Misconceptions (What Quality Circles are Not?)

- Quality Circles do not tackle just quality problems.
- Quality Circle is not a substitute or replacement for task forces, product committees, joint plant councils or works committees, quality assurance department, suggestion schemes.
- Quality Circles do not change the existing organizational structure or the chain of command.
- Quality Circles are not a forum for grievances or a springboard for demands.
- Quality Circles are not a means for the management to unload all their problems.
- Quality Circles are not just another technique or fad.
- Quality Circles are not a panacea for all ills.

Pitfalls and Problems

- Lack of faith in and support to Quality Circle activities among management personnel.
- Inadequate training to the concerned people.
- Lack of interest or incompetence of leaders/facilitator(s).
- Apathy, fear and misunderstanding among middle level executives.
- Delay or non-implementation of Circle recommendations.
- Irregularity of Quality Circle activities.
- Non-application of simple techniques for problem solving.
- Lack of participation or non-participation by some members in the Circle activities.
- Circles running out of problems.
- Inadequate visibility of management support.
- Non-maintenance of Quality Circle records.
- Too much facilitation or too little.
- Feeling of inadequacy of decision-making authority or delegation among QC participants.
- Language difficulty in communication.

- Communication gap between Circles and departmental head.
- Change of management.
- Confusing Quality Circle for another technique.
- Resistance from trade unions.

Structure of Quality Circles Program

Six Basic Elements

1. Circle participants or members.
2. Circle leaders/deputy leaders.
3. Program facilitator(s).
4. Steering/advisory committee.
5. Top management.
6. Potential members and non-participating management/members.

Roles and Responsibilities of Various Elements

Roles of Members

- Focus on organizational objectives through the theme(s) selected for one's Quality Circle.

- Theme/problem should be related to work.
- Do not bring in the personal issues or problems as the themes of Quality Circles.
- Demonstrate mutual respect.
- Take training in all the aspects of Quality Circles.
- Acquire the necessary skills in various Quality Circle tools and techniques.
- Participate wholeheartedly in problem solving process by giving ideas and views voluntarily and suggesting the solutions.
- Attend all the meetings of Quality Circle. When unavoidable to attend the meeting, seek prior permission of the Quality Circle leader.
- Participate in implementing the finalized solutions.

Roles of Leaders

- Decide date and time of each Quality Circle meeting and inform to all the members.
- Ensure maximum attendance of all the members in the meetings.
- Conduct the meetings effectively.

- Motivate the members for their full participation in the proceedings of Quality Circle meetings and related activities.
- Facilitate the members in data collection.
- Maintain the records of Quality Circle meetings and other related activities.
- Interact with other Quality Circle leaders.
- Interact with the Quality Circle facilitator frequently.
- Make presentations of solutions to the management. Involve the members in making the presentations.
- Seek management approvals of the solutions.
- Ensure implementation of the approved solutions with the active involvement of the members.
- Arrange first time training and later on, the refresher training of the members and self in the Quality Circles group process, tools and techniques.

Roles of Facilitators

- Act as an effective link between the Quality Circles and the management.
- Coordinate the work of several Quality Circles through their respective leaders.

- Act as a resource person for the Quality Circles being facilitated.
- Arrange for obtaining necessary expertise from other agencies and Quality Circles.
- Keep the motivation and morale level of all the leaders and members at the highest level.
- Review the progress of each Circle periodically and lead them appropriately.
- Continually update the knowledge and skills pertaining to the working of Quality Circles by studying the relevant literature and attending the training programs.
- Transfer the knowledge and skills to the leaders and the members.
- Arrange for additional training to the leaders and members as required.
- Arrange for necessary monetary budgets and keep the required records.
- Facilitate and guide the Quality Circle leaders and members to make the management presentations.

Roles of Steering Committee (Management)

- Formally announce the launching of Quality Circle

initiative in the organization.

- Provide full support and encouragement to Quality Circle movement in the organization.
- Provide leadership and guidance to develop the Quality Circle models, structure and policies.
- Design the opportunities for presentations by the Quality Circles.
- Facilitate the approval and implementation of the solutions presented by Quality Circles.
- Sanction the necessary monetary budgets for smooth working of Quality Circles.
- Provide the logistic support as needed (presentation venues, meeting rooms, time, finance, training facilities etc).
- Plan out and execute various training programs for the existing and prospective Quality Circle facilitators, leaders and members.
- Give due recognition to Quality Circles, their members and their work by way of prizes, felicitations and other monetary and non-monetary means.
- Develop guidelines for measuring the effectiveness of Quality Circles and also the Quality Circle initiative as a whole.

- Review the performance and progress of Quality Circles periodically.

How Do Quality Circles Operate?

1. Appointment of a steering committee, facilitator(s) and QC team leaders.
2. Formation of QCs by nomination/voluntary enrolment of QC members.
3. Training of all QC members (by an expert consultant and trainer).
4. Training of non-participating employees (by an expert consultant and trainer).
5. Building a problem data bank and identification of problems for QC work.
6. QC problem resolution by QCs through standardized techniques.
7. Presentation of QC solutions to management.
8. Evaluation of Quality Circles for bestowing appropriate award/recognition and reward.

Code of Conduct for QCs

- Attend all meetings and be on time.

- Listen to the views of other members and show respect.
- Make others feel a part of the group.
- Criticize ideas, not persons.
- Help other members to participate more fully.
- Be open to and encourage the ideas of others.
- Every member is responsible for the team's progress.
- Maintain a friendly attitude.
- Strive for enthusiasm.
- The only stupid question is the one that is not asked.
- Look for merit in the ideas of others.
- Pay attention- avoid disruptive behavior.
- Avoid actions that delay progress.
- Carry out assignments on schedule.
- Give credit to those whom it is due.
- Thank those who give assistance.
- Do not suppress ideas- do express.
- Objectives and causes first, solutions next.
- Give praise and honest appreciation when due.
- Ideas generated by the group should not be used as individual suggestions to suggestion scheme of the organization.

Quality Circle Presentations: Important Aspect

Periodic presentations by the Quality Circles are an important aspect of the QC system. Members and team leaders under the guidance of facilitators prepare and rehearse their presentations. The presentation is broken down into logical segments and members/leader take their turn to present a particular part of presentation assigned to each.

The presentations are normally made to the departmental managers or to the top management/steering committee and at times to specific invitees for the following purposes:

1. To seek management's confirmation on selection of the problem(s).
2. To report the progress of their work on the selected problem(s).
3. To get the approval of the management on the solutions suggested by them by presenting the benefits and the required investments.
4. To inform the management on their plan of implementation of the solutions.

5. To keep the concerned authorities updated on the status of implementation and the actual benefits accrued.

6. To seek suggestions from the audience for bringing about improvements in their working as Quality Circles.

7. To thank the agencies and people who assisted and supported them in their work.

It is important to train the circle members, leaders and facilitators to impart them the necessary presentation skills.

Problem Solving Tools and Techniques Used by Quality Circles (Old QC Tools)

Given below are the most commonly used tools and techniques. These are called the old QC tools:

1. Brainstorming: It is used to create many ideas by using brains of various individuals in a group.

2. Pareto analysis: It is used for sifting out important (significant) from unimportant (insignificant) enabling you to act on important factors as the first priority.

3. Cause and effect diagram (or fishbone diagram or Ishikawa diagram): It is used to identify the probable reasons for an effect or an outcome and classify them into useful categories and subcategories.

4. Histogram: This graph or pictorial presentation is used for showing frequency distribution i.e. how often each different value in a set of data occurs.

5. Scatter diagram: This graph shows pairs of data, one variable on each axis in order to study the relationship between them.

6. Stratification: It is used to separate data gathered from a variety of sources so that patterns can be seen.

7. Check sheet: It is a structured and well-designed form to collect the data and later analyze it.

8. Control charts and graphs: These are used to study the processes and their capabilities by determining if the processes are operating within control limits.

New QC Tools

Quality Circles started using additional seven tools as they started maturing in the use of the conventional (old) QC tools mentioned earlier. These new QC tools are:

1. Relation diagram: It is used to find appropriate solution strategies by using the technique called why why analysis (also known as 5 why analysis).
2. Affinity diagram: It is used to reduce the number of ideas from a long list of ideas to a workable number by group consensus process.
3. Systematic diagram or Tree diagram: It is used to develop a succession of strategies to achieve an objective logically and systematically.
4. Matrix diagram: It is used to enable the data based on the ideas to be deployed effectively to examine the relationships.
5. Matrix data analysis diagram: It is used to find the importance of the task in a constrained resource situation.
6. PDPC (Process Decision Program Chart): It is used to plan and design the activities needed to solve a problem when the information is incomplete or vague or the situation is fluid and hard to forecast.
7. Arrow diagram: It is used to plan the order of operations, their sequence, relationship and criticality in time schedule.

Benefits of QC

- Self-development.
- Promotes leadership qualities among participants.
- Promotes problem solving attitude and skills among the participants.
- Recognition.
- Participants feel that they are participating in the organizational work more meaningfully.
- Achievement satisfaction.
- Promotes group/team working resulting in better synergies.
- Serves as cementing force between management/non-management groups.
- Promotes continuous improvement in products and services.
- Brings about a change in environment of more productivity, better quality, reduced costs, safety and corresponding rewards.
- Improves the overall organizational culture.
- Thus provides more value to the customers.

Awards and Rewards to the Participants of Quality Circles

It is important to understand that for formation, sustenance and growth of Quality Circles in an organization, the participants (members, leaders, facilitators/coordinators etc) should be constantly motivated by the management of the organization.

For this purpose it is necessary to give monetary and non-monetary awards and rewards to the participants. Some practices followed by various organizations are given below:

Non-monetary Awards

- Public felicitations.
- Dinners with dignitaries.
- Prizes.
- Picnics and excursions with family members of the participants.
- Mention of achievements in the media.
- Deputation to national and international Quality Circles conferences.

Monetary Rewards

- One time lump sum payment.
- Cost savings based payments.
- Annual bonus.
- Rise in salary by linking the achievement of quality circle participants to the formal performance evaluation system of the organization.

Importance of Training for Success of Quality Circles

Success of entire Quality Circles movement rests on the quality and quantity of training imparted to all the concerned people from the grass root level to the top most level.

Organizations and institutions should design, develop and timely conduct the awareness, detailed and need based customized programs.

The often-conducted programs are:

- Awareness or orientation program.

- Program for top management.

- Program for other levels of management.

- Program for QC steering committee members.

- Program for QC facilitators.

- Program for circle leaders.

- Program for QC members.

- In-depth program in QC tools and problem solving techniques.

- Program on written communication and report writing.

- Program on spoken/verbal communication with inputs of transactional analysis.

- Program on presentation skills.

- Program on group dynamics, group process and conducting QC meetings.

- Program to train the QC trainers.

Quality Circles System: An Ongoing System

The best part of Quality Circles system is that it can be used in every organization perennially. It is not a one time or short-term fad.

Organizations keep facing the problems from time to time and they need to solve them. And if they could achieve it by involving their people at various levels particularly including the grass root level through Quality Circles, not only the problems will be solved better and expeditiously but it will also boost the motivation and morale of the people. Organizations can thus expect to gain better synergies.

Appendix

Detailed History (Compete History of Evolution of Quality Circles)

Statistical Quality Control

1947: General Douglas McArthur requested US Government to send experts to help Japanese rejuvenate their industries. Dr Edward Deming was sent.

1949: An Overseas Technical Research Committee was organized by the Union of Japanese Scientists and Engineers (JUSE)

1949: JUSE organized a seminar on "SQC"

1949: JUSE organized a seminar "Quality Control- Basic Course"

1950: JUSE published a magazine "SQC"

1950: Dr Deming invited to eight day Quality Control seminar organized by JUSE

1951: Deming prize instituted

1954: Dr Joseph Juran invited to Quality Control Management seminar organized by JUSE

1956: Japan's radio started broadcasting a Quality Control Course organized by JUSE

1960: Japanese Government declared November as Quality

Month and Q-flag was adopted

Quality Control Circles or Quality Circles

Quality Control Circles (Japan)

1962: First QC Circle was registered with QC Circle Head Quarters

1962: First annual QC Conference for Foremen was held

1964: Regional chapters of QC Circles were organized in four different districts

1966: Dr Juran observed Japanese QC Circle activities

1966: Special QC Circle session was organized at the 10th conference of European Organization for Quality Control held in Stockholm, Sweden

1967: Number of registered QC Circles grew to 10000

1968: JUSE dispatched the first QC Circle Study Team overseas

1969: Registered Circles grew to 20000

1969: 100th QC Circle Conference was held in Tokyo

1970: Registered Circles grew to 30000

1971: JUSE organized the first QC Circle seminar

1971: 200th QC conference was held

1971: Registered QC Circles grew to 40000

1971: First National QC Circle Conference was held in Tokyo

1972: Regional Circles grew to 50000

1973: 300th QC Circle Conference was held

1974: Registered circles grew to 60000

1974: 400th QC Circle conference was held

1975: Registered Circles grew to 70000. 500th Conference was held

1977: Registered Circles grew to 80000. 700th Conference was held

1978: Registered Circles grew to 90000

1978: First international QC Circle Convention was held

1979: 800th QC Circle Conference was held

1979: Registered QC Circle Conference numbered 100000

1980: 900th Conference was held

1981: International QC Circle Convention was held

1985: Third International QC Circle Convention was held

1988: More than one million Circles with over ten million members

Quality Circles (Other than Japan)

Quality Circles (USA)

1974: Lockheed Company, USA started Quality Circle movement

1977: International Association of Quality Circles (IACC) was formed in USA

1980: 230 companies in USA had Quality Circles

1983: There were more than 500,000 known Quality Circles active in the world

Quality Circles (India)

1980: BHEL, Hyderabad first in India to start Quality Circles

1982: Quality Circle Forum of India (QCFI) was founded

1983: Tata Motors (formerly Telco), Pune, India started Quality Circles by 1985 they had more than 400 Circles at one time

1985: BHEL had 1411 Circles covering around 13362 members

www.ingramcontent.com/pod-product-compliance
Lightning Source LLC
Chambersburg PA
CBHW051303170526
45165CB00004B/1835